SANJEEV KAPOOR

VEGETARIAN RECIPES FROM MARWAR

In association with Alyona Kapoor

Popular Prakashan
www.popularprakashan.com

Published by
POPULAR PRAKASHAN PVT. LTD.
301, Mahalaxmi Chambers
22, Bhulabhai Desai Road
Mumbai - 400 026
for KHANA KHAZANA PUBLICATIONS PVT. LTD.

First Published 2013

(4342)
ISBN: 978-81-7991-783-1

Design: Anjali Sawant
Photography: Bharat Bhirangi

PRINTED IN INDIA
by Sai Print 'o' Pack
New Delhi - 110 020

AUTHOR'S NOTE

The Marwari vegetarian cuisine is rich in taste and full of distinct flavours. Depending on the availability of the ingredients in the region, various spices and herbs like dried mango powder, mustard seeds and asafoetida are used in the masala and cooked in pure ghee. Due to the non-availability of the fresh vegetables all the year round, gram flour is a major ingredient in regional favourites like *kadhi*, *gatte ki sabzi*, *pakodi*. Powdered lentils are used to make *mangodi* and *papad*. With the scarcity of water, the cuisine's speciality is that it uses minimum water, while maximising on milk, buttermilk and ghee as cooking fluids.

In *Vegetarian Recipes from Marwar*, enjoy the crispy *Katori Chaat* and *Corn Pakore*, the hearty *Masaledar Karele* and fragrant *Kesariya Baingan*; the nutritious *Gond Ke Laddoo* and delicious *Aloo ka Halwa*, to name a few.

Happy Cooking!

Sanjeev Kapoor

CONTENTS

ACCOMPANIMENTS

DESSERTS

DAHI KE KABAB

½ cup yogurt

5 French beans, boiled and mashed

½ cup green peas, boiled and mashed

9 small potatoes, boiled, peeled and mashed

2 tablespoons oil + for deep-frying

1 inch ginger, chopped

2 green chillies, chopped

1 teaspoons *garam masala* powder

1 ½ tablespoons chopped fresh coriander

1 teaspoons salt

2½ tablespoons cornflour

1 cup breadcrumbs

Heat two tablespoons oil in a non-stick pan. When small bubbles begin to appear at the bottom of the pan, add the ginger and green chilles and sauté for one minute.

Add the mashed French bean and green pea and sauté for two minutes.

Add the potatoes, *garam masala* powder, chopped coriander and salt.

Mix well and take the pan off the heat. Set aside to cool.

Add the cornflour to the cooled potato mixture and mix well. Divide into eight equal portions and shape into balls.

Divide the yogurt into eight equal portions. Moisten your hands and flatten each portion of the potato mixture into a small disc.

Place one portion of yogurt in the centre, bring in the edges together and seal ensuring that the yogurt is completely covered with the potato mixture.

Roll into a ball and press lightly. Make the rest of the kababs similarly. Place the breadcrumbs in a plate and roll the kababs in it so that they are well covered with the breadcrumbs all around.

Heat the oil in a non-stick *kadai* and deep-fry the kababs until golden brown.

Drain on absorbent paper.

Serve hot with a chutney of your choice.

Chef's Tip: This is not the traditional recipe but it tastes just as good when prepared in this manner.

CORN PAKORE

250 grams fresh corn kernels

2 teaspoons green chilli paste

1½ teaspoons ginger paste

1 teaspoon *chaat masala*

1 teaspoon coriander powder

2 tablespoons chopped fresh coriander

5-6 tablespoons gram flour

Salt to taste

Oil for deep-frying

Coarsely grind the corn and place in a large bowl. Add the green chilli paste, ginger paste, *chaat masala*, coriander powder, chopped coriander, gram flour and salt. Mix well.

Heat sufficient oil in a non-stick *kadai*. Drop small portions of the corn mixture into the hot oil and deep-fry the *pakore* till golden brown on both sides.

Drain on absorbent paper.

Serve hot with Green Chutney (page 94).

ALOO KE SOOLEY

500 grams medium potatoes, parboiled and halved lengthways

6 tablespoons gram flour

1 tablespoon rice flour

2 teaspoons red chilli powder

1 teaspoon turmeric powder

5-6 green cardamoms

1 tablespoon roasted coriander seeds

1 teaspoon roasted cumin seeds

4 tablespoons yogurt

Salt to taste

Pure ghee, as required

In a large bowl, combine the gram flour, rice flour, chilli powder and turmeric powder.

Grind the green cardamoms, coriander seeds and cumin seeds to a powder. Add to the gram flour mixture and mix well.

Add the yogurt, salt and two to three tablespoons of water and mix thoroughly. Add the potatoes and marinate for thirty minutes.

Preheat the oven to 200°C/400°F/Gas Mark 6.

Thread the potato halves onto metal or wooden skewers and cook in the oven, basting occasionally with ghee, till golden brown. Serve with Green Chutney (page 94).

DAL SAMOSA

¾ cup skinless split green gram
½ cup refined flour
4 green chillies
3 cloves
2 teaspoons fennel seeds
4-5 black peppercorns
1 inch ginger, chopped
4 tablespoons ghee
A generous pinch of asafoetida
½ teaspoon cumin seeds
1 teaspoon red chilli powder
Salt to taste
2 teaspoons *chaat masala*
Oil for deep-frying

Soak the green gram in three cups of water for two hours. Drain and grind coarsely using very little water.

Grind the green chillies, cloves, fennel seeds, peppercorns and ginger to a paste.

Heat two tablespoons of ghee in a non-stick *kadai*; add the asafoetida and cumin seeds. When the seeds begin to change colour, add the chilli powder and coarsely ground gram.

Sauté for three or four minutes and add the green chilli paste and salt.

Cover the pan and cook till the gram is soft. Sprinkle a little water occasionally to prevent scorching.

Add the *chaat masala* and mix well. Remove from heat and set aside to cool. Divide into eight portions.

Sift the refined flour with a little salt. Rub in two tablespoons of hot ghee. Add enough water and knead to make a stiff dough.

Divide into four portions and roll each one out into a thin oval-shaped *chapati*. Cut in half and fold into a cone.

Fill with a portion of the green gram mixture and seal the open edges.

Heat sufficient oil in a non-stick *kadai* and deep-fry the *samosa* on medium heat till golden brown and crisp. Drain on absorbent paper.

Serve hot with Date and Tamarind Chutney (page 94).

KANJI BADA

Kanji

1¼ tablespoons brown mustard seeds, coarsely ground

½ teaspoon red chilli powder

1½ teaspoons black salt

Bada

½ cup skinless split green gram, soaked

A pinch of asafoetida

½ teaspoon coriander seeds, coarsely powdered

½ teaspoon fennel seeds, coarsely powdered

¼ teaspoon green chilli paste

1½ tablespoons chopped fresh coriander

A pinch of baking powder

½ teaspoon table salt

8 black peppercorns, crushed

Oil for deep-frying

For the *kanji*, combine coarsely ground mustard seeds, chilli powder and black salt in a deep bowl. Add two and a half cups of water. Mix well; cover with a lid and set aside for about two days to ferment.

Taste to see if it has turned sour. Once the water turns sour place the mixture in the refrigerator.

For the *bada*, wash and soak the green gram in one and a half cups of water for three hours. Drain and place in a blender and grind to a smooth paste without adding any extra water.

Transfer the paste into a large bowl. Add the asafoetida, coarsely powdered coriander and fennel seeds, chilli paste, chopped coriander, baking powder, salt and crushed peppercorns and mix well.

Whisk the batter with your hands for ten to fifteen minutes to incorporate air and make the batter light.

Heat the oil in a non-stick *kadai*. Drop tablespoonful of batter into the hot oil and deep-fry till golden brown on all sides. Drain on absorbent paper and cool.

Soak the fried *bada* in one and a half cups of water for five minutes. Squeeze gently and dip them in the *kanji*. Cover with a lid and place in the refrigerator for two hours.

Serve chilled.

MIRCHI BHAJIYA

8 large green chillies, slit and seeded

¾ cup gram flour

¾ teaspoon baking powder

¼ teaspoon asafoetida

¾ teaspoon red chilli powder

1½ teaspoons salt

1 tablespoon oil + for deep-frying

½ teaspoon mustard seeds

4-5 garlic cloves, crushed

¼ teaspoon turmeric powder

2 large potatoes, boiled, peeled and mashed

Place the gram flour, baking powder, asafoetida, chilli powder, three-fourth teaspoon salt and one cup of water in a deep bowl and whisk well to make a smooth batter. Set aside the batter for about ten minutes.

Heat one tablespoon oil in a medium non-stick pan on medium heat. When small bubbles appear at the bottom of the pan, add the mustard seeds.

When they begin to splutter add the garlic and sauté on medium heat till fragrant. Add the turmeric powder and the mashed potatoes and mix well.

Add three-fourth teaspoon salt and mix. Take the pan off the heat and set aside to cool.

Divide the mixture into eight equal portions and stuff each portion into each slit chillies.

Place a non-stick *kadai* on high heat and pour in the remaining oil. When small bubbles appear at the bottom of the *kadai*, reduce the heat to medium.

Dip each chilli in the gram flour batter and gently slide them into the hot oil. Cook four chillies at a time.

Cook, turning the chillies with a slotted spoon a few times, for four to five minutes or till they turn golden and crisp. Drain on absorbent paper.

Serve immediately.

KACHCHE KELE AUR MATAR KE CUTLET

5-6 medium unripe bananas, boiled and mashed

½ cup shelled green peas, boiled and mashed

3 green chillies, finely chopped

A pinch of asafoetida

½ teaspoon red chilli powder

½ teaspoon dried mango powder

1 teaspoon *garam masala* powder

2 tablespoons chopped fresh coriander

Salt to taste

Oil for shallow-frying

Place the mashed bananas and green peas in a deep bowl.

Add the green chillies, asafoetida, chilli powder, dried mango powder, *garam masala* powder, chopped coriander and salt and mix well.

Divide into sixteen equal portions and shape into round or heart shaped cutlets.

Heat the oil in a non-stick pan and shallow-fry the cutlets till light golden brown. Drain on absorbent paper.

Serve hot with Date and Tamarind Chutney (page 94).

PEANUT CHAAT

2 cups raw peanuts
1 tablespoon sea salt
1 teaspoon turmeric powder
Salt to taste
¼ teaspoon *chaat masala*
½ teaspoon red chilli powder
1 teaspoon roasted cumin powder
1 medium onion, chopped
1 medium tomato, chopped
2 green chillies, chopped
2 tablespoons chopped fresh coriander
2 tablespoons lemon juice

Place the peanuts with five cups of water, sea salt and turmeric powder in a pressure cooker and pressure-cook till the pressure is released four to five times (four to five whistles).

Remove the lid when the pressure reduces. Cool, drain and shell the peanuts.

Place the peanuts in a bowl. Add salt, the *chaat masala,* chilli powder, roasted cumin powder, onion, tomato, green chillies, chopped coriander, and lemon juice and mix well.

Serve hot or cold.

KATORI CHAAT

Katori

5 medium potatoes

2 tablespoons cornflour

Salt to taste

Oil for deep-frying

Filling

1 cup chickpeas, soaked

Salt to taste

2 tea bags

2 tablespoons ghee

2 medium onions, chopped

1 teaspoon ginger paste

1 teaspoon garlic paste

4 tablespoons *chole masala*

¾ cup tomato purée

4 tablespoons chopped fresh coriander

To Serve

4 tablespoons thick yogurt

2 tablespoons Date and Tamarind Chutney (page 94)

2 tablespoons Green Chutney (page 94)

4 tablespoons *sev*

2 tablespoons chopped fresh coriander

Grate the potatoes coarsely and soak them in six cups of water for five minutes.

Drain on absorbent paper. Transfer to a bowl, add the cornflour and a little salt and mix well. Divide into four portions.

Take two small strainers – one slightly larger than the other. Heat sufficient oil in a non-stick *kadai*.

For each *katori*, layer the larger strainer with one portion of the grated potatoes. Place the other strainer over the potato layer and press lightly.

Gently lower both the strainers together into the hot oil and deep-fry till the potatoes are golden. Drain on absorbent paper and set aside.

To make the filling, drain the chickpeas, and place in a pressure cooker with three cups of water, salt and the tea bags.

Pressure-cook till the pressure is released five to six times (five to six whistles) till the chickpeas are soft.

Drain, reserving one-fourth cup of cooking liquid, and set aside.

Heat two tablespoons of ghee in a deep non-stick pan on medium heat; add the onions and sauté till golden. Add the ginger paste and garlic paste, and sauté for half a minute.

Lower the heat, add three tablespoons of *chole masala* and continue to sauté for another minute.

Add the tomato purée and cook for three to four minutes. Add the chickpeas along with the reserved stock and simmer for three to four minutes till the ghee rises to the surface.

Sprinkle the remaining *chole masala* and chopped coriander, stir and cover immediately. Keep the chickpeas warm.

Fill the chickpeas into each of the fried *katori*. Drizzle one tablespoon of yogurt and top with tamarind chutney and green chutney. Sprinkle the *sev* and chopped coriander, and serve immediately.

MOONG DAL CHEELA

1¼ cups split green gram with skin

1½ inches ginger, roughly chopped

5-6 garlic cloves, roughly chopped

1 medium onion, roughly chopped

3 green chillies, roughly chopped

Salt to taste

¼ teaspoon red chilli powder

Oil, as required

¾ cup Green Chutney (page 94)

¾ cup cottage cheese, grated

Soak the gram in three cups of water for about half an hour. Drain and grind with the ginger, garlic, onion, green chillies and salt to make a smooth batter. Add the chilli powder and mix well.

Heat a non-stick *tawa* and grease it with oil. Spread a ladleful of batter with the back of the ladle into a thin round. Drizzle a little oil and cook on medium heat till the underside is cooked. Carefully flip the *cheela* over, drizzle a little oil and cook the other side too.

Spread some green chutney over the *cheela*. Sprinkle the cottage cheese and fold the *cheela* over into a half-moon shape. Serve hot.

LAPSI TIKKI

½ cup broken wheat
1 cup shelled green peas
1 green chilli, chopped
2 teaspoons *chaat masala*
½ cup chopped fresh coriander
2 tablespoons lemon juice
6 garlic cloves, chopped
Salt to taste
Cornflour, for dusting
Oil for deep-frying

Soak the broken wheat in one cup of hot water for half an hour. Drain and put it into a food processor or blender.

Add the green peas, green chilli, *chaat masala*, chopped coriander, lemon juice, garlic and salt, and grind together.

Transfer the mixture to a bowl. Divide into sixteen equal portions and shape each one into a *tikki*. Roll the *tikki* in the cornflour.

Heat sufficient oil in a non-stick *kadai* and deep-fry the *tikki* till golden brown. Drain on absorbent paper. Serve hot with Green Chutney (page 94) or tomato ketchup.

Note: *You can also shallow-fry the tikki for a healthier option.*

PALAK PAPDI CHAAT

20 large fresh spinach leaves

20 crisp flat *puri*, crushed

½ cup gram flour

¼ teaspoon carom seeds

2 teaspoons red chilli powder

Salt to taste

Oil for deep-frying

2 medium potatoes, boiled and chopped

2-3 tablespoons Date and Tamarind Chutney (page 94)

2 tablespoons Green Chutney (page 94)

1 teaspoon dried mango powder

1 teaspoon roasted cumin powder

1 teaspoon *chaat masala*

½ teaspoon rock salt

¼ cup yogurt, whisked and chilled

1 cup *sev*

2 tablespoons fresh pomegranate kernels

2 tablespoons chopped fresh coriander

In a large bowl, mix the gram flour, carom seeds, chilli powder and salt.

Add enough water to make a thick batter.

Heat the oil in a non-stick *kadai* on medium heat. Dip and coat individual spinach leaves in the gram flour batter, and deep-fry in hot oil.

Drain on absorbent paper. Cut each *palak* pakora in half.

Place the *palak pakore* in a serving dish, and top with the crushed *puri* and potatoes.

Drizzle date and tamarind chutney and green chutney over.

Sprinkle dried mango powder, cumin powder, *chaat masala* and rock salt.

Drizzle yogurt and top with the *sev*, pomegranate kernels and chopped coriander and serve immediately.

ARBI KA KHATTA SHAAK

250 grams colocasia tubers, boiled, peeled and sliced
1 cup yogurt
2 teaspoons gram flour
1 teaspoon coriander powder
1 teaspoon red chilli powder
1 teaspoon dried mango powder
½ teaspoon *garam masala* powder
Salt to taste
1½ tablespoons ghee
½ teaspoon carom seeds
A pinch of asafoetida
1 teaspoon ginger paste
2 teaspoons garlic paste
2 tablespoons chopped fresh coriander

Whisk together the yogurt, gram flour, coriander powder, chilli powder, dried mango powder, *garam masala* powder and salt.

Heat the ghee in a non-stick pan; add the carom seeds and asafoetida, and sauté for ten seconds. Add the sliced colocasia and sauté on medium heat till light brown.

Add the ginger and garlic pastes, and sauté for two minutes.

Add the yogurt mixture and cook on medium heat till most of the moisture dries up and the gravy thickens.

Garnish with the chopped coriander and serve hot.

ALOO KA RASSAWALA SHAAK

4 medium boiled potatoes, cut into ½-inch pieces
1 cup yogurt
1 tablespoon gram flour
Salt to taste
¼ teaspoon turmeric powder
1 tablespoon pure ghee
½ teaspoon cumin seeds
A pinch of asafoetida
7-8 curry leaves
½ inch ginger, chopped
2 green chillies, chopped
¼ teaspoon red chilli powder
½ teaspoon *garam masala* powder

Whisk the yogurt with the gram flour, salt and turmeric powder. Add three-fourth cup of water and mix well.

Heat the ghee in a non-stick pan. Add the cumin seeds and when they begin to change colour, add the asafoetida, curry leaves, ginger and green chillies. Sauté for a minute. Add the chilli powder and yogurt mixture, and mix well.

Add the potatoes and cook, stirring continuously, till the mixture comes to a boil. Lower the heat and simmer for five to six minutes. Sprinkle with the *garam masala* powder and serve hot.

BHARWAN GATTE

2½ cups gram flour

2 cups yogurt, whisked

1½ teaspoons red chilli powder

½ teaspoon turmeric powder

1 teaspoon ginger paste

Salt to taste

¼ teaspoon soda bicarbonate

½ cup grated cottage cheese

½ cup grated *khoya/mawa*

4 green chillies, chopped

2 tablespoons oil

1 teaspoon cumin seeds

¼ teaspoon fenugreek seeds

8-10 black peppercorns

3 dried red chillies, broken into large bits

A pinch of asafoetida

½ teaspoon *garam masala* powder

2 tablespoons chopped fresh coriander

Whisk the yogurt with two cups of water, two tablespoons of gram flour, the chilli powder and turmeric powder.

Mix the remaining gram flour with the ginger paste, salt and soda bicarbonate. Add enough water and knead well to make a stiff dough. Set aside for five minutes.

In a bowl, mix together the grated cottage cheese, *khoya*, half the green chillies and salt. Divide into sixteen equal portions.

Divide the gram flour dough into sixteen equal portions.

Flatten each portion and stuff it with one portion of the cottage cheese-*khoya* mixture. Shape into cylinders.

Cook the stuffed *gatte* in boiling water for ten to fifteen minutes. Drain and cut into one-inch pieces. Heat the oil in a non-stick *kadai*; add the cumin seeds and stir-fry till they change colour. Add the fenugreek seeds, peppercorns, red chillies, remaining green chillies and asafoetida, and sauté for a minute.

Add the whisked yogurt, and cook, stirring continuously, for three to four minutes, until the gravy thickens slightly. Add the *garam masala* powder, and adjust the seasoning. Add water if required. Add the cooked *gatte* to the gravy and continue cooking till the gravy thickens.

Garnish with the chopped coriander and serve hot.

CHANE JAISALMER KE

1½ cups black Bengal gram

1½ cups yogurt

4 teaspoons gram flour

¼ teaspoon turmeric powder

Salt to taste

1 teaspoon red chilli powder

2 teaspoons coriander powder

1 teaspoon *garam masala* powder

3-4 green chillies chopped

4 tablespoons pure ghee

A pinch of asafoetida

1 teaspoon cumin seeds

2 tablespoons chopped fresh coriander

Soak the black Bengal gram overnight or for six hours, in four cups of water.

Drain; add four cups of water and pressure-cook till tender with a little salt.

Drain and reserve the cooking liquid. Mash the gram lightly.

In a separate bowl, mix together the yogurt, gram flour, turmeric powder, salt, chilli powder, coriander powder and *garam masala* powder, and whisk well till smooth.

Add the green chillies and mix. Add one cup of the reserved liquid and mix again.

Heat the ghee in a non-stick pan; add the asafoetida and cumin seeds.

When the cumin seeds begin to change colour, add the yogurt mixture and stir.

Add the cooked gram, adjust the seasoning and add some of the reserved liquid.

Bring to a boil and cook for five minutes.

Garnish with the chopped coriander and serve hot.

DAHI PAPAD KI SABZI

1½ cups sour yogurt

3 *Bikaneri moong papad*

¾ tablespoon gram flour

½ teaspoon turmeric powder

¾ teaspoon red chilli powder

Salt to taste

1½ tablespoons pure ghee

1 teaspoon cumin seeds

1½ teaspoons coriander powder

½ teaspoon asafoetida

2 dried red chillies, broken into large bits

¾ cup *boondi*

1 tablespoon chopped fresh coriander

½ teaspoon *garam masala* powder

In a large bowl, combine the yogurt, gram flour, turmeric powder, chilli powder and salt. Add two cups of water and mix well. Strain and set aside.

Heat the ghee in a non-stick *kadai* and add the cumin seeds. When they change colour, add the coriander powder and sauté for one minute.

Add the asafoetida and red chillies, and sauté for half a minute.

Add the yogurt mixture and adjust the seasoning. Stir continuously till the mixture comes to a boil. Lower the heat and simmer for two minutes.

Heat a non-stick *tawa* and roast the *papad* on both sides. Break them roughly into two-inch pieces.

Add the *papad* and *boondi* to the simmering yogurt mixture and cook for two or three minutes.

Garnish with the chopped coriander and *garam masala* powder. Serve hot.

KESARIYA BAINGAN

A large pinch of saffron threads, finely crushed

1 large (800 grams) brinjal

3 tablespoons oil

1 large onion, chopped

2 garlic cloves, crushed

1 inch ginger, chopped

1 teaspoon cumin seeds

⅔ cup drained (hung) yogurt

2 tablespoons mango chutney (with small cubes of mango)

Salt to taste

Black pepper powder to taste

2 tablespoons chopped fresh coriander

Place the saffron threads in a small bowl; add boiling water and leave to infuse for five minutes.

Trim the stalk of the brinjal, cut lengthways into quarters, then into half-inch thick slices.

Heat the oil in a large non-stick frying pan; add the onion and sauté for three minutes. Add the brinjal, garlic, ginger and cumin seeds and stir gently for three minutes.

Stir in the saffron-infused water, yogurt and mango chutney, and cook on a low heat for eight to ten minutes, stirring frequently, until the brinjal is cooked through and tender.

Season with salt and pepper powder, garnish with the chopped coriander and serve hot.

GUAR KI SABZI

200 grams cluster beans, stringed and broken into small pieces

4 pieces of dried mango

2 tablespoons oil

1 teaspoon cumin seeds

2 dried red chillies, broken

A large pinch of asafoetida

1 teaspoon mustard powder

1 teaspoon salt

6 tablespoons yogurt, whisked

2 teaspoon red chilli powder

1 teaspoon turmeric powder

2 tablespoons *garam masala* powder

2 teaspoons coriander powder

Soak the dried mango pieces in one-fourth cup of water for half an hour.

Heat the oil in a non-stick pan on low heat. When small bubbles appear at the bottom of the pan, add the cumin seeds, broken red chillies, asafoetida and mustard powder and stir for one minute.

Add the cluster beans and salt. Mix well and add the yogurt.

Mix together the chilli powder, turmeric powder, *garam masala* powder and coriander powder in a bowl and add one-fourth cup of water and mix.

Add this mixture to the pan and mix. Add the dried mango pieces along with the water in which they were soaked and mix. Cook for ten minutes or till dry.

Serve hot.

Note: *This is a popular dish from Rajasthan.*

DAHIWALE AMRUD

4 medium guavas, seeded and cut into small pieces

½ cup yogurt

½ tablespoon coriander powder

¼ teaspoon red chilli powder

¼ teaspoon turmeric powder

1 teaspoon dried mango powder

1 tablespoon ghee

2 green chillies, chopped

½ teaspoon cumin seeds

½ teaspoon fennel seeds

¼ teaspoon asafoetida

1 medium tomato, chopped

Salt to taste

¼ teaspoon *garam masala* powder

½ teaspoon sugar

Whisk the yogurt with all the powdered spices, except the *garam masala* powder.

Heat the ghee in a non-stick *kadai*; add the green chillies, cumin seeds, fennel seeds and asafoetida, and stir to mix.

Add the whisked yogurt, tomato and salt, and stir for a while.

Add three-fourth cup of water and bring to a boil. Add the guavas and let the gravy come to a boil again.

Lower the heat, cover and cook, stirring occasionally, till the guavas are cooked.

Add the *garam masala* powder and cook for another three or four minutes.

Sprinkle the sugar and stir. Serve hot.

KER SANGRI

1½ cup desert berries
1 cup dried desert beans
1 cup + 4 teaspoons yogurt, beaten
Salt to taste
2 tablespoons oil
1 teaspoon cumin seeds
5-6 dried red chillies, broken into large bits
2 teaspoons ginger paste
½ teaspoon turmeric powder
1 teaspoon red chilli powder
1 teaspoon coriander powder
5-6 pieces of dried mango
1 teaspoon dried mango powder
1 tablespoon chopped fresh coriander

Soak the berries and dried beans in one cup of beaten yogurt overnight. Remove from the yogurt and wash under running water.

Boil them for fifteen to twenty minutes in two cups of water with salt. Drain.

Heat the oil in a non-stick *kadai*; add the cumin seeds, red chillies and ginger paste, and sauté till the cumin seeds change colour. Add a little water, turmeric powder, chilli powder and coriander powder, and stir. Add the dried mango pieces and four teaspoons of yogurt, and mix well.

Add the berries and beans to the pan, and mix. Add the salt, dried mango powder and chopped coriander, and mix well. Serve hot.

MASALEDAR KARELE

8 medium bitter gourds
2¾ teaspoons salt
4 large onions, peeled
3½ tablespoons fennel seeds
2 teaspoons coriander powder
2 teaspoons cumin powder
¾ teaspoon turmeric powder
1½ tablespoons dried mango powder
¾ tablespoon red chilli powder
½ tablespoon *garam masala* powder
¾ cup oil
1 tablespoon sugar
1 green chilli, stemmed and slit

Scrape the skins of the bitter gourds. Slit each one lengthways, without cutting through and remove the seeds. Rub salt all over and set aside for half an hour. Squeeze lightly and wash under running water. This removes the bitterness to a great extent. Wipe dry.

Add one-fourth teaspoon salt to the gourd scrapings and set side for thirty minutes. Squeeze tightly.

Finely chop two onions and slice the remaining two.

Place a small non-stick *kadai* on low heat and add the fennel seeds and dry-roast for thirty seconds. Grind the roasted fennel seeds to a fine powder. Transfer into a small bowl and add coriander powder, cumin powder, turmeric powder, dried mango powder, chilli powder and *garam masala* powder and mix well.

Place a medium non-stick pan on medium heat and pour in three tablespoons oil. When small bubbles appear in the oil add the chopped onions and sauté for six to eight minutes or till golden.

Take the pan off the heat and add the spice mix, one and a half teaspoons salt and sugar. Divide into eight portions.

Stuff one portion of this mixture into each of the slit bitter gourds and set them aside

Place a non-stick pan on medium heat and pour in the remaining oil. When small bubbles appear at the bottom of the pan, add the sliced onions, green chilli and the bitter gourd scrapings and sauté for three to four minutes.

Neatly arrange the stuffed bitter gourds over this mixture. Reduce heat to low, cover and cook, for fifteen to twenty minutes or till the gourds and cooked and tender.

While cooking gently turn the gourds a few times so that they get evenly browned all around. Serve hot.

MOOLI SAAG

4 medium white radishes with leaves
Salt to taste
2 tablespoons oil
½ teaspoon mustard seeds
½ teaspoon cumin seeds
A pinch of asafoetida
½ teaspoon turmeric powder
1 teaspoon red chilli powder
1½ teaspoons sugar
1 teaspoon dried mango powder

Chop the radishes into small pieces. Shred the leaves. Sprinkle a little salt on the radishes and set aside for twenty minutes. Drain the liquid.

Heat the oil in a non-stick *kadai* and add the mustard seeds. When they begin to splutter add the cumin seeds and asafoetida, and sauté for half a minute.

Add the turmeric powder and chilli powder, and sauté for ten seconds. Add the radishes with the leaves, and sauté for a minute. Sprinkle a little water to prevent scorching. Cover and cook on medium heat for ten minutes or till the radishes are soft and tender.

Sprinkle the sugar and dried mango powder, and mix well. Adjust seasoning. Serve hot with the *paranthe*.

KHASTA KACHORI

2 cups refined flour

Salt to taste

½ teaspoon soda bicarbonate

5 tablespoons oil + for deep-frying

Filling

½ cup skinless split black gram, soaked

3 tablespoons pure ghee

1 inch ginger, finely chopped

1 green chilli chopped

A pinch of asafoetida

1 teaspoon coriander powder

½ teaspoon cumin powder

1 teaspoon red chilli powder

¼ teaspoon fennel powder

6-8 cashew nuts, roughly chopped

1 tablespoon raisins

½ teaspoon sugar

Salt to taste

1 tablespoon lemon juice

Sift the flour, salt and soda bicarbonate together in a bowl. Add the oil and mix well. Knead with a little water to make a soft dough. Cover with a damp cloth and set aside.

For the filling, coarsely grind the soaked split black gram with a little water.

Heat the ghee in a non-stick *kadai*; add the ground *dal*, ginger, green chilli, asafoetida, coriander powder, cumin powder, chilli powder, fennel powder, cashew nuts and raisins. Sauté till all the moisture has dried up.

Stir in the sugar, salt and lemon juice. Remove from heat and set aside to cool. Divide into sixteen portions.

Divide the dough into sixteen equal balls. Roll out each one into a small *puri*, thinner at the edges and thicker in the centre.

Place a portion of filling in the centre and bring the edges together to form a ball.

Heat sufficient oil in a non-stick *kadai* and deep-fry the *kachori* on low heat for three to five minutes, or until golden brown and crisp. Drain on absorbent paper.

Serve with Date and Tamarind Chutney (page 94).

MAWA KAJU MATAR

⅔ cup *mawa/khoya*, crumbled
12 cashew nuts, ground
2¾ cups green peas, shelled
2 tablespoons oil
½ teaspoon red chilli powder
2 teaspoons coriander powder
¾ teaspoon fennel powder
½ teaspoon *garam masala* powder
3 medium tomatoes, chopped
Salt to taste
2 green chillies, chopped
2 tablespoons chopped fresh coriander

Heat the oil in a heavy-bottomed non-stick pan. Add the *mawa* and sauté on low heat, stirring continuously, till it changes colour.

Add the chilli powder, coriander powder, fennel powder, *garam masala* powder, and mix well.

Add the tomatoes and salt, and cook till the tomatoes soften. Add the cashew nut paste and continue to sauté for one minute.

Add the green peas and green chillies. Add one cup of water and cook till the oil separates. Serve hot, garnished with chopped coriander.

BESAN CHEELA RAITA

¾ cup gram flour

2 cups thick yogurt, whisked

1 teaspoon red chilli powder

½ teaspoon cumin seeds

¼ teaspoon powdered mustard seeds

Salt to taste

A pinch of soda bicarbonate

1 teaspoon oil + for shallow-frying

1 teaspoon sugar

A pinch of asafoetida

1 tablespoon chopped coriander

In a bowl, combine the gram flour, half the chilli powder, the cumin seeds, powdered mustard seeds and salt to taste.

Add enough water to make a thick batter. Whisk thoroughly to remove lumps.

Add the soda bicarbonate and whisk well.

Heat a non-stick *tawa* and apply a little oil. Drop small spoonfuls of the gram flour batter on the *tawa* and shallow-fry the small *cheele* using more oil if needed. Fry till golden brown on both sides.

Add half a cup of water to the yogurt and add the remaining chilli powder, the sugar and salt to taste. Add the *cheele* to the yogurt.

Heat a teaspoon of oil in a small non-stick pan and add the remaining cumin seeds.

When they begin to change colour, add the powdered mustard seeds and asafoetida.

Remove from heat immediately and pour over the yogurt.

Serve at once, garnished with the chopped coriander.

RAJASTHANI KADHI

Pakore

1 cup gram flour

A pinch of soda bicarbonate

2 green chillies, chopped

½ teaspoon red chilli powder

½ teaspoon carom seeds

½ teaspoon turmeric powder

½ teaspoon coriander powder

Salt to taste

Oil for deep-frying

Kadhi

2 cups sour yogurt

2 tablespoons gram flour

Salt to taste

¾ teaspoon turmeric powder

1 tablespoon oil

½ teaspoon cumin seeds

A pinch of asafoetida

2-3 green chillies, chopped

1 inch ginger, chopped

10-12 curry leaves

½ teaspoon red chilli powder

For the *pakore*, mix together all the ingredients, except the oil, with one-fourth cup of water.

Heat the sufficient oil in a non-stick *kadai*; drop small portions of the *pakore* mixture into the hot oil and deep-fry till golden brown. Drain on absorbent paper and set aside.

For the *kadhi*, mix together the yogurt, gram flour, salt and turmeric powder, and whisk well till smooth.

Heat the oil in a non-stick *kadai* and add the cumin seeds. When they begin to change colour, add the asafoetida, green chillies and ginger, and sauté for one minute.

Add the curry leaves, chilli powder and the yogurt mixture. Bring to a boil and cook, stirring continuously, till thick.

Stir in the *pakore* and serve hot with rice.

RAJASTHANI PANCHMEL DAL

¼ cup split Bengal gram
¼ cup whole green gram
¼ cup skinless split black gram
¼ cup split pigeon peas
¼ cup whole red lentils
1½ teaspoons salt
½ teaspoon turmeric powder
3 tablespoons oil
¼ teaspoon asafoetida
½ teaspoon cumin seeds
4-5 cloves
2 dried red chillies, stemmed and broken into 2 pieces
½ teaspoon green chilli paste
½ teaspoon ginger paste
1 teaspoon roasted cumin powder
1 teaspoon coriander powder
1 teaspoon red chilli powder
3 medium tomatoes, chopped
½ teaspoon *garam masala* powder
2 tablespoons chopped fresh coriander

Combine the pulses in a bowl and wash them two to three times. Soak the pulses in three cups of fresh water for at least two hours.

Boil in four cups of water in a non-stick pan with one teaspoon salt and the turmeric powder. Reduce the heat to medium, add the drained *dal* and cook, uncovered, for twenty-five minutes or till the *dal* is done.

Heat the oil in another non-stick pan; add the asafoetida, cumin seeds, cloves and red chillies. When the cumin seeds begin to change colour, add the chilli paste and ginger paste and sauté for one minute.

Add the cumin powder, coriander powder and chilli powder and stir well. Add the tomatoes and cook for eight to ten minutes or till oil separates.

Add the cooked *dal* with the cooking liquid, half a teaspoon salt and one and a half cups of water. Cook for ten minutes, stirring well.

Add the *garam masala* powder and stir. Garnish with chopped coriander and serve hot with Bati (page 61).

RAJASTHANI BATI

2 cups whole-wheat flour

¼ teaspoon baking powder

2 teaspoons salt

⅔ cup + 6 tablespoons pure ghee

½ teaspoon carom seeds

Preheat oven to 220°C/425°F/Gas Mark 7.

In a bowl mix together flour, baking powder and salt. Sift and keep aside.

Rub two-third cup of ghee into the flour mixture till it resembles breadcrumbs. Add carom seeds and three-fourth cup of water and knead to a dough.

Divide the dough into eight portions and shape them into small balls. Bake them for about ten minutes.

Lower heat to 200°C/400°F/Gas Mark 6 and continue to bake for another thirty-five minutes. Place six tablespoons of pure ghee in a microwave-safe bowl and melt it in a microwave for one minute on HIGH.

Remove the *bati* from the oven, press them lightly and soak them in the melted pure ghee for at least one hour.

Remove from bowl before serving and serve with Rajasthani Panchmel Dal (page 59) and pure ghee.

Chef's Tip: Traditionally *bati* are baked on cowdung cake fire.

RAJASTHANI MOTIYAN PULAO

1 cup cottage cheese, grated

3 tablespoons cashew nut powder

1½ tablespoons cornflour

1½ cups Basmati rice

Salt to taste

Oil for deep-frying

2 sheets edible silver foil

1 tablespoon ghee

6-8 cloves

2 bay leaves

2 one-inch cinnamon sticks

6-8 green cardamoms

A few saffron strands

¼ cup raisins

Wash and soak rice in four cups of water for about half an hour. Drain and set aside.

Place the grated cottage cheese in a bowl. Add the cashew nut powder, cornflour and salt. Knead into a smooth dough and roll into small balls.

Heat sufficient oil in a non-stick *kadai* and deep-fry on medium heat till light golden brown.

Drain on absorbent paper. When cool, wrap in edible silver foil.

Heat the ghee in a non-stick *kadai*; add the cloves, bay leaves, cinnamon and cardamoms, and sauté till fragrant.

Add the rice and stir gently for one minute. Add three cups of hot water, saffron, raisins and salt.

When the mixture comes to a boil, lower the heat, cover and cook till the rice is done.

Serve rice in a platter, garnished with the fried cottage cheese balls.

TIKADIA

1½ cups whole-wheat flour

Salt to taste

6 tablespoons pure ghee + to serve

1 teaspoon roasted cumin seeds

½ teaspoon red chilli powder

1 medium onion, chopped

½ medium tomato, chopped

2 teaspoons chopped fresh coriander

In a large bowl, combine the wheat flour, salt and four tablespoons of ghee. Add sufficient water and knead to make a soft dough. Divide the dough into four equal portions.

In a bowl, combine the cumin seeds, chilli powder, onion, tomato and chopped coriander. Divide the mixture into four portions.

Roll out each portion of dough into a thick three-inch disc and apply a little ghee on it. Place a portion of the onion-tomato mixture in the centre.

Sprinkle a little salt. Gather the edges together and seal. Press and roll out into a thick *roti*.

Heat a non-stick *tawa* and cook the *roti* on medium heat till golden brown on both sides.

Serve hot, topped with a dollop of ghee.

JODHPURI VEGETABLE PULAO

12 small cauliflower florets

¼ cup shelled fresh green peas

15 cashew nuts, halved

10 almonds, halved

4-5 dried dates, chopped

1 tablespoon raisins

1½ cups Basmati rice, soaked and drained

5 tablespoons pure ghee

1 teaspoon cumin seeds

½ teaspoon fennel seeds

1 tablespoon ginger paste

1 tablespoon garlic paste

Salt to taste

¾ cup yogurt

½ teaspoon *garam masala* powder

10-12 black peppercorns, crushed

Heat four tablespoons of ghee in a deep non-stick pan. Add the cumin seeds and fennel seeds, and sauté till fragrant.

Add the cashew nuts, almonds and dried dates, and sauté for a minute.

Add the cauliflower, ginger paste, garlic paste, raisins and salt, and sauté for another minute.

Stir in the rice and yogurt, and mix. Add two cups of water and the *garam masala* powder, and mix well.

When the mixture comes to a boil, lower heat, cover and cook till the rice is half done.

Add the green peas and stir to mix. Cover and cook on medium heat till tender.

Sprinkle the crushed peppercorns and drizzle with the remaining ghee. Stir gently and serve hot.

BIKANERI DAL PARANTHE

1¼ cups split Bengal gram, soaked

1½ cups refined flour + for dusting

Salt to taste

6 tablespoons pure ghee

¼ teaspoon asafoetida

1 teaspoon coriander powder

1 teaspoon red chilli powder

½ teaspoon *garam masala* powder

Oil for shallow-frying

Combine the refined flour, salt and four tablespoons of ghee. Add sufficient water and knead to make a soft, smooth dough. Cover with a damp cloth and rest the dough for ten minutes.

Pressure-cook the split Bengal gram with two cups of water and salt till the pressure is released two or three times (two or three whistles).

Remove the lid when the pressure reduces completely and set the gram aside to cool. Grind to a coarse paste.

Heat the remaining ghee in a non-stick *kadai*.

Add the asafoetida, coriander powder, chilli powder and *garam masala* powder. Sauté for half a minute.

Add the ground gram and cook for three to four minutes or till dry. Adjust the seasoning and mix well.

Remove from heat and allow to cool. Divide into eight portions and set aside.

Divide the dough into eight portions and roll into balls.

Shape each portion on your palm into a small *puri*; place a portion of stuffing in the centre, gather up the edges and shape into a ball again.

Press each ball down lightly on the tabletop. Roll out into a thin *parantha*, dusting with flour if required. The *parantha* should be as thin as a *papad*.

Heat sufficient oil in a non-stick pan. Slide a *parantha* gently into the oil and shallow-fry till evenly golden brown on both sides.

Drain on absorbent paper and serve hot.

BESAN KI MASALA ROTI

Roti

1 cup gram flour

½ cup wholewheat flour

Salt to taste

2 tablespoons pure ghee
+ for shallow-frying

Filling

1½ teaspoons cumin powder

½ teaspoon coriander powder

¼ teaspoon turmeric powder

1 green chilli, chopped

Salt to taste

½ teaspoon dried mango powder

½ teaspoon red chilli powder

1½ tablespoons pure ghee

Combine all the ingredients for the filling in a small bowl. Set aside.

Combine all the ingredients for the *roti* and knead into a soft dough using water as required.

Divide the dough into eight portions and shape into balls.

Roll out each ball into a four-inch disc and place one-fourth of the *masala* filling on it.

Fold in half and then again in half to make a triangle.

Roll out to make a triangular *roti*.

Heat a non-stick *tawa* and fry each *roti* with a little ghee till both sides are golden brown.

Spread a little ghee on the *roti* and press it gently between your palms. Serve hot.

MOOLI BAJRA ROTI

3 medium radishes, grated

2 cups millet flour + for dusting

Salt to taste

1 small onion, finely chopped

2 green chillies finely chopped

1 teaspoon red chilli powder

1 teaspoon ginger paste

1 teaspoon dried mango powder

½ teaspoon *garam masala* powder

2 tablespoons finely chopped coriander

Ghee for shallow-frying

Mix some salt into the grated radish and set aside for half an hour. Squeeze tightly to remove excess moisture.

In a deep bowl, mix together the radish, millet flour, onion, green chillies, chilli powder, ginger paste, dried mango powder, *garam masala* powder, chopped coriander and salt thoroughly.

Add sufficient warm water and knead into a dough.

Divide the dough into eight equal portions and roll into balls. Lightly dust each ball with flour, place on a plastic sheet and pat with your fingers into a thick *roti*.

Heat a non-stick *tawa* and place the *roti* on it.

Cook for a while, then flip the *roti* over and drizzle some ghee all around.

Flip the *roti* over again and drizzle some more ghee all around and cook till both sides are cooked and golden brown.

Serve hot with a dollop of ghee.

Chef's Tip: Do not rest the dough as the radish will release water and make the dough sticky.

MOONG DAL PURI

½ cup skinless split green gram, soaked

1½ cups whole-wheat flour

3 tablespoons oil + for deep-frying

1 teaspoon ginger paste

1 teaspoon red chilli powder

½ teaspoon coriander powder

¼ teaspoon cumin powder

¼ teaspoon *garam masala* powder

Salt to taste

Drain and coarsely grind the green gram.

Heat two tablespoons of oil in a non-stick pan. Add the ginger paste and sauté for half a minute on medium heat.

Add the chilli powder, coriander powder, cumin powder and *garam masala* powder, and sauté for half a minute.

Add the salt and ground gram, and sauté for three to four minutes. Set aside to cool.

Place the whole-wheat flour in a deep bowl. Add the salt, one tablespoon of oil and sufficient water and knead into a soft dough.

Cover with a damp cloth and rest the dough for fifteen minutes. Divide both the dough and the stuffing into eight portions each.

Take each portion of the dough in your palm and spread it slightly.

Place a portion of stuffing in the centre, gather in the edges and roll into a ball. Roll out into a three-inch *puri*.

Heat sufficient oil in a non-stick *kadai* and deep-fry the *puri*, one by one, till lightly browned.

Drain on absorbent paper and serve hot with yogurt.

GOR KERI

1 kg grated jaggery

1 kg unripe mangoes, peeled and cut into ½-inch cubes

6 teaspoons salt

1 teaspoon turmeric powder

200 grams pickle *masala* (see below)

1 tablespoon fennel seeds

Add the salt and one teaspoon turmeric powder to the mango cubes in a large glass bowl and mix well.

Cover and set aside for five to six hours. During this time the mango cubes will release water.

Drain the mango cubes, spread them on a large plate and dry in the sun for about six hours.

Place the dried mango cubes in a large glass bowl. Add the jaggery, pickle *masala* and fennel seeds and mix well.

Cover and set aside for six to eight days stirring twice daily till all the jaggery has melted.

Store in sterilised airtight glass or porcelain jars.

PICKLE MASALA

100 grams split mustard seeds, lightly roasted

100 grams crushed fenugreek seeds, lightly roasted

100 grams split coriander seeds, lightly roasted

300 grams red chilli powder

½ teaspoon turmeric powder

1 teaspoon asafoetida

¼ cup oil

To make the pickle *masala*, heat the oil to smoking point. Take it off the heat and set aside to cool completely.

Combine together the split mustard seeds, fenugreek seeds, split coriander seeds, chilli powder, turmeric powder and asafoetida and mix well.

Add the oil and mix again. You can store this in an airtight jar to be used when required.

TEEKHA NIMBU ACHAAR

6 large lemons, quartered and seeded

¼ cup salt

½ cup sugar

2 inches ginger, crushed

2-3 tablespoons red chilli powder

2 star anise, roasted

1 tablespoon roasted mustard seeds

1 teaspoon roasted fenugreek seeds

8 green chillies, chopped

Place the lemons in a large bowl and sprinkle salt all over.

Cover and leave to stand for one day. On the following day, toss the lemons in the brine.

Squeeze the juice of four pieces of salted lemons in a small non-stick pan.

Add the sugar, ginger, chilli powder, star anise and three tablespoons of water.

Bring to a boil, lower the heat and simmer, stirring continuously, till the sugar dissolves completely.

Pound together the roasted mustard seeds, fenugreek seeds and green chillies.

Add to the mixture. Cook for one minute longer; remove from heat and set aside to cool.

Pour the remaining lemon quarters into a sterilised glass jar.

Pour the cooled spice mixture over the lemons, pressing them down so that they are completely covered.

Cover the jar with a lid and leave to stand for fifteen to twenty days for the pickle to *mature.*

KERI KI LAUNJEE

1 kilogram unripe green mangoes
3 tablespoons mustard oil
¾ teaspoon fenugreek seeds
4 teaspoons fennel seeds
½ teaspoon onion seeds
1 teaspoon coriander powder
1 teaspoon red chilli powder
½ teaspoon turmeric powder
Salt to taste
1¼ cups grated jaggery

Peel the mangoes, cut them lengthways into quarters and remove the seeds.

Heat the oil in a non-stick *kadai* to smoking point. Lower the heat to medium, add the fenugreek seeds and sauté till they begin to change colour.

Add the fennel seeds, onion seeds, coriander powder, chilli powder, turmeric powder and salt, and mix well. Add the mangoes and sauté for five minutes.

Add the jaggery and half a cup of water. Bring to a boil, cover the *kadai*, lower the heat and simmer, stirring occasionally, for seven to eight minutes. Remove from the heat and set aside to cool. Store in sterilised bottles when completely cold.

GOND KE LADDOO

100 grams edible gum crystals, broken into small pieces

100 grams ghee

50 grams almonds, coarsely powdered

50 grams dried dates, coarsely powdered

2 tablespoons grated dried coconut

1 tablespoon poppy seeds

¼ teaspoon nutmeg powder

150 grams jaggery

Heat the ghee in a non-stick *kadai* and fry the gum pieces till they fluff up like popcorn. Cool and crush to a coarse powder.

Dry-roast almonds, dates, coconut and poppy seeds till fragrant and mix them with gum powder. Add nutmeg powder and mix.

Melt jaggery and cook to make a syrup of one-string consistency.

Add the syrup to the above mixture and mix everything well.

Immediately roll into *laddoo*, cool completely and store.

MALPUA

1 litre milk

1¼ cups sugar

6-8 saffron strands

¼ cup + 1 teaspoon refined flour

1 tablespoon semolina

2 cups pure ghee + for shallow-frying

Boil the milk in a heavy-bottomed non-stick pan till it reduces to a consistency that coats the back of a spoon. Remove from heat and set aside to cool.

Reserve two tablespoons of sugar. Place the remaining sugar in a deep non-stick pan, add half cup of water and cook on medium heat, stirring occasionally.

Add two teaspoons of milk. Collect the scum with a ladle and discard. The sugar syrup will now be clear.

Cook till the sugar syrup reaches one-string consistency .

Soak the saffron threads in a teaspoon of hot milk and add it to the sugar syrup.

Stir the refined flour, semolina and the reserved sugar into the cooled thickened milk. Mix well and make a batter of pouring consistency, adding a little milk if required.

Set aside for three hours. Do not refrigerate the batter.

Heat the ghee in a wide-mouthed, flat-bottomed *kadai*.

Pour a little batter into the hot ghee to form a pancake.

Ladle hot ghee over the pancake for one minute and turn it over.

When both sides are cooked, drain and immerse in the saffron-flavoured sugar syrup for at least fifteen minutes.

Serve warm.

Chef's Tip: To check if the sugar syrup has reached a one-string consistency, place a drop of the syrup between your thumb and forefinger and slowly pull them apart. If the syrup forms a single string then the syrup is ready.

CHURMA

2 cups whole-wheat flour

4 tablespoons semolina

½ cup melted pure ghee + for deep-frying + to serve

Milk, as required

¾ cup powdered sugar

¼ teaspoon green cardamom powder

10 cashew nuts, chopped

10 almonds, chopped

10 raisins

Mix the flour and semolina in a bowl. Add half a cup of melted ghee and mix well. Add sufficient milk and knead into a stiff dough.

Divide the dough into twelve lemon-sized balls.

Heat sufficient ghee in a non-stick *kadai* and deep-fry the balls on medium heat, till they are cooked through. Drain on absorbent paper and cool.

Coarsely grind the wheat balls in a processor. Transfer to a bowl, add the powdered sugar, cardamom powder, cashew nuts, almonds and raisins and mix well. Serve the *churma* with ghee.

ALOO KA HALWA

6 medium potatoes, boiled, peeled and grated

½ cup ghee

1 cup milk

1½ cups powdered sugar

1 teaspoon green cardamom powder

½ cup assorted nuts, chopped

Heat the ghee in a heavy-bottomed pan.

Add the grated potatoes and sauté well. The more you sauté the better the *halwa* tastes.

Stir continuously as it tends to stick to the bottom a little.

Add the milk and powdered sugar, and mix well.

Cook till the sugar dissolves completely and the ghee starts to separate.

Add the cardamom powder and assorted nuts, and mix well.

Serve warm.

AAMRAS WITH KESAR

1 kg ripe mangoes

¼ teaspoon saffron strands, roasted and crushed

1 cup sugar, powdered

2½ cups milk, chilled

Remove the pulp from the mangoes. Pass through a thin piece of muslin.

Add the powdered sugar and the chilled milk. Stir in the saffron. Serve chilled.

MAWA GUJIYA

Pastry Covering

2 cups refined flour

3 tablespoons ghee + for deep-frying

Filling

2½ cups *khoya/mawa*, grated and roasted

3¼ teaspoons desiccated coconut

15 cashew nuts, chopped

15 almonds, blanched and chopped

20 raisins

A pinch of nutmeg powder

¼ teaspoon green cardamom powder

2½ cups powdered sugar

½ cup grated chocolate

For the pastry covering, sift the flour and rub in three tablespoons of ghee.

Add cold water and knead to make a stiff dough. Cover it with a damp cloth and set aside.

Place the *khoya* in a bowl and add the desiccated coconut, cashew nuts, almonds, raisins, nutmeg powder and cardamom powder and mix well.

Add the powdered sugar and the grated chocolate and mix again.

With greased hands divide the dough into small balls. Grease the *gujiya* mould.

Roll out each ball of dough balls into a small *puri*; place in the mould and press down lightly. Place the stuffing in the hollow portion.

Moisten the edges with a little water, close the mould and press firmly. Open the mould and remove the extra dough. Cover the *gujiya* with a damp cloth.

If you do not have a mould, roll out each *puri* and cut with a *katori* to make a perfect circle. Place the stuffing on one half, lightly moisten the edges and fold the other half over the stuffing and press the edges firmly, using a fork to make a design.

Heat sufficient ghee in a *kadai* and deep-fry the *gujiya* on medium heat till golden brown. Drain on absorbent paper.

Leave to cool slightly before serving, as the filling will be very hot.

BASIC RECIPES

Green Chutney

Grind together 1 cup fresh coriander, ½ cup fresh mint, 2-3 green chillies, black salt to taste, ¼ teaspoon sugar and 1 tablespoon lemon juice to a smooth paste using a little water if required.

Date and Tamarind Chutney

Wash, stone and chop 15-20 dates. Dry-roast 2 teaspoons cumin seeds and ¼ teaspoon fennel seeds. Cool and grind to a powder. Cook the dates, 1 cup tamarind pulp, cumin and fennel powder, ½ cup jaggery, 2 teaspoons red chilli powder, 1 teaspoon dried ginger powder, black salt, salt and four cups of water till thick.

GLOSSARY

English	Hindi
Almonds	Badam
Asafoetida	Hing
Banana, unripe	Kachcha kela
Bay leaf	Tej patta
Bengal gram, split	Chana dal
Bengal gram, whole black	Kale chane
Black gram, skinless, split	Dhuli urad dal
Black peppercorns	Kali mirch
Broken wheat	Dalia
Cardamom, green	Chhoti elaichi
Carom seeds	Ajwain
Cashew nuts	Kaju
Chickpeas	Kabuli chana
Cinnamon	Dalchini
Cloves	Laung

English	Hindi
Cluster beans	Guar phalli
Coconut, dried	Khopra
Colocasia tubers	Arbi
Coriander seeds	Dhania
Corn kernels	Makai ke dane
Cottage cheese	Paneer
Cumin seeds	Jeera
Curry leaves	Kadhi patta
Dried dates	Chuare
Dried mango powder	Amchur
Fennel seeds	Badi Saunf
Fenugreek seeds	Methi dana
French beans	Farsi
Fresh coriander	Taazi hari dhania

English	Hindi	English	Hindi
Gram flour	Besan	Pigeon peas, split	Arhar dal/ toovar dal
Green gram, skinless split	Dhuli moong dal	Pomegranate kernels	Anar ke dane
Green gram, split	Chilkewali moong dal	Poppy seeds	Khus khus
Green gram, whole	Sabut moong	Raisins	Kishmish
Green peas	Taaze matar	Red lentils, whole	Sabut masoor
Jaggery	Gur	Refined flour	Maida
Mango, unripe, green	Keri	Rock salt	Sendha namak
Millet	Bajra	Saffron	Kesar
Mustard seeds	Rai	Semolina	Sooji/rawa
Nutmeg	Jaiphal	Star anise	Chakri phool/ badiyan
Onion seeds	Kalonji	Whole-wheat flour	Atta
Peanuts, raw	Kachche moongphalli	Yogurt	Dahi